RITES OF PASSAGE

AN IN-DEPTH LOOK AT INDIA'S 16 SACRED CEREMONIES"

DR. JAGADEESH PILLAI

|| "Dedicated to all who seek to understand and appreciate Indian culture and tradition." ||

Contents

Contents

Prayer

**"Om Poornamadah Poornamidam Poornat
Poornamudachyate,Poornasya Poornamaadaya
Poornamevavashishyate,Om Shantih, Shantih, Shantih"**

*The literal interpretation of this mantra is: That which is
Absolute, This which is Absolute, Absolute arises from Absolute,
If Absolute is removed from Absolute, Absolute remains
OM Peace, Peace, Peace.*

🙏🙏🙏

About The Author

Dr. Jagadeesh Pillai is a renowned Guinness World Record holder, writer, and researcher hailing from Varanasi, also known as the abode of Lord Shiva. With a Ph.D. in Vedic Science and a range of creative ideas and achievements, he is a true polymath. He is the author of more than 100 books including Research Publications. Although his roots can be traced back to Kerala, the people of Varanasi hold him in high regard and affectionately consider him one of their own.

Dr. Pillai has achieved four Guinness World Records in the following subjects:

"Script to Screen" - In this record, Dr. Pillai produced and directed an animation film within the shortest time possible, breaking the previous record set by Canadians. He has also received numerous national and international awards and recognitions for this achievement.

Longest Line of Postcards - For this record, Dr. Pillai created a line of 16,300 postcards on the occasion of the 163rd anniversary of Indian Postal Day. The event also included a questionnaire about the Indian flag.

Largest Poster Awareness Campaign - Dr. Pillai designed an awareness campaign on the subject of "Beti Bachao - Beti Padhao" (Save the Girl Child - Educate the Girl Child) to achieve this record.

Largest Envelope - In tribute to the Indian Prime Minister's

"Make in India" initiative, Dr. Pillai created a 4000 square meter envelope using waste paper to achieve this record.

Attempted - **70000 Candles on a 210 kg Cake** - To celebrate the 70th Indian Independence Day, Dr. Pillai attempted to light 70,000 candles on a 210 kg cake, which was recorded in World Records India.

Attempted - **Documentary on Dhamek Stupa of Sarnath in 17 Languages** - Dr. Pillai attempted to create a documentary on the Dhamek Stupa of Sarnath, dubbing it in 17 different languages. The result of this attempt is currently awaiting confirmation from the Guinness World Records.

Dr. Pillai is skilled in teaching the Bhagavad Gita, a Hindu scripture, and is popular among young people. He has helped many young people improve their lives through his motivational teachings.

In addition to teaching, he has composed and sung numerous Sanskrit Bhajans and patriotic songs.

He has also written and directed several short films and documentaries for awareness campaigns, and has volunteered with the police in both UP and Kerala to spread awareness about various issues through videos and photography.

Incredibly, he has produced and directed over 100 documentaries about the city of Varanasi, all on his own.

He has also helped and guided more than 25 boys and girls to achieve world records through creative and innovative methods. He is a multifaceted person who uses his intellect and the blessings given to him by God to excel in various areas. He is both a teacher and a student, always learning and teaching, and is able to master any subject he comes across.

He is a selfless social activist and motivational speaker who has overcome struggles and failures to become a successful and enthusiastic individual with a rich life experience.

In addition to his work with the Bhagavad Gita, he is also an efficient Tarot card reader, Astro-Vastu consultant, and a talented singer and composer. He has sung the entire Ram Charita Manas and Bhagavad Gita in his own compositions, and has sung the phrase "Lokah Samastha Sukhino Bhavantu" in 50 different languages. He is currently working on a detailed and scientific study of Vedas, Upanishads, Puranas, and the Bhagavad Gita. He has also composed and sung the Hanuman Chalisa and Gayatri Mantra in 108 and 1008 different compositions, respectively.

Awards - Four Times Guinness World Records, Winner of Mahatma Gandhi Vishwa Shanti Puraskar, Mahatma Gandhi Global Peace Ambassador, Kashi Ratna Award, Dr. APJ Abdul Kalam Motivational Person of the Year 2017, Mother Teresa Award, Indira Gandhi Priyadarshini Award, Bharat Vikas Ratna Award, Udyog Ratna Award, Vigyan Prasar Award, Poorvanchal Ratn Samman.

ᢒᢒᢒ

Preface

The book "Shodasha Samskaras: 16 Rites of Passage of Indian Tradition" delves into the rich cultural heritage of India, specifically focusing on the 16 rites of passage that mark important milestones in an individual's life. From birth to death, these samskaras play a significant role in shaping one's identity and connecting them to the community and tradition.

The book provides a comprehensive and in-depth examination of each samskara, including their historical and cultural context, rituals, and significance. It also explores the ways in which these rituals have evolved over time and how they continue to shape modern Indian society.

The book is intended for readers with an interest in Indian culture and tradition, as well as those studying anthropology, sociology, and religious studies. The book is written in an accessible style, making it suitable for both the general reader and the academic audience.

The authors of the book have put a great effort in research, gathering information from various texts, and consulting with experts in the field, to bring together a comprehensive and accurate representation of the 16 samskaras. We hope that this book will not only inform readers about the customs and traditions of India, but also inspire them to appreciate the rich cultural heritage of our country.

ৡৡৡ

Prologue

Shodasha Samskaras : 16 Rites of Passage

Samskaras are ceremonies or rituals in Hinduism and other Indian religions that mark important momentsin a person's life. The word "samskara" means "putting together" or "making perfect" in ancient Sanskrit. The term Samskara is derived from two Sanskrit words: 'sams' and 'kara'. The former translates to 'inward', and the latter as 'action'. Thus, this tradition comes from the concept of 'inward action,' a ritualistic act of offering safety, peace, and prosperity to an individual.

In the context of karma theory, samskaras are dispositions or traits that exist in a person's subconscious from birth or that are developed over a lifetime. These traits influence a person's behavior and states of mind.

Samskaras also refer to the sacraments in Hinduism, Jainism, Buddhism and Sikhism. The number and details of these sacraments vary depending on regional traditions. They can include both external rituals like a baby's birth and name-giving ceremony, as well as inner rites of resolution and ethics like compassion towards all living beings and a positive attitude.

Samskara is an important concept in Hinduism and refers to the various life events and rituals performed during an individual's lifespan that effect the person's spiritual growth. Your samskaras are said to shape your life and influence how one lives out their dharma, or life's purpose.

At birth, a person traditionally receives the jaatakarma samskara, wherein they are given a blessing of luck and a drop of honey in their mouths, followed by the namakarana or naming ceremony. During this samskara, the child's name is chosen and announced before the community and the child is formally welcomed into society. The samskara of upanayanam is a coming of age ritual usually performed at the age of 8 for boys and 12 for girls, during which time the student begins formal study of Vedic texts under the guidance of a Guru.

The next important samskara is vivaha, or marriage, which involves a sacred ceremony to celebrate the union of two people. Both the bride and groom also receive special mantras to be said every day for their continued happiness and prosperity. The next two samskaras focus on family life: garbha-dharanam Sarkara, or the ritual gifting of pregnancy, and punyaha-vachnam, or the ritual of purifying and granting blessings on the new home of the couple or their family.

Following punyaha-vachnam, Hindu adults now participate in the samskara of snaana-dharanam, or the ritual of taking a bath before attending festivals and other holy occasions. Other samskaras during this stage of life include chudakarman and manyasaras, which is the tonsure of a boy's head. Moving onto adulthood, the next important samskara is the samavartana for students, whereupon they receive their degrees and offer the guru their gratitude marking the end of their formal education.

The grhasta-asrama samskara follows soon after, which

involves the householder understanding their role as the head of the household and is served as a recognition of one's maturity into adulthood. Then there is vedarambha samskara, which is the vedic initiation for boys to begin their study of the Vedas and other ancestral scriptures. This is followed by antyeshti samskara, the last of the samskaras and the funeral ceremony that symbolizes the liberation of the soul from the body.

Samskaras are an integral part of Hinduism and the various milestones that mark spiritually significant periods. They are an important step in a person's spiritual development and journey towards self-realization and enlightenment.

ᐳᐳᐳ

Disclaimer

"The names and rituals of the 16 samskaras, or rites of passage, in Indian tradition may vary across different regions and communities in India. This book presents the most commonly used names and rituals for these samskaras."

ᐅᐅᐅ

ONE
GARBHADANA SAMSKARA

Garbhadana Samskara – is performed by a married couple when conceiving a child. This important Samskara raises the act of conception to a sacred occasion, and is powerfully purifying and uplifting for the unborn child.

Shodasha Samskaras are a set of 16 religious rites of passage that are an important part of Hindu culture. These ceremonies, which span a person's entire life, are designed to help individuals progress spiritually and fulfill their duties and obligations to society. The first of these 16 Samskaras is the Garbhadana Samskara, which is performed by a married couple when they are conceiving a child.

The Garbhadana Samskara is considered to be a very important ceremony, as it raises the act of conception to a sacred occasion. It is believed that by performing this ritual, the couple is able to purify themselves and create a favorable environment for the unborn child. The ritual also helps to create a strong spiritual bond between the parents and the child, and it is said to have a powerful uplifting effect on the child's soul.

The exact rituals and ceremonies that make up the Garbhadana Samskara can vary depending on the specific traditions and practices of different regions and communities. However, some common elements that are usually included are:

Puja (worship) of the deities who are associated with procreation and fertility, such as Lord Shiva and Parvati.

Chanting of specific mantras and prayers, which are believed to have a purifying and uplifting effect.

Offering of various symbolic gifts and offerings to the deities, such as flowers, fruits, and grains.

Lighting of lamps, which is said to symbolize the kindling of the fire of spiritual life in the unborn child.

Following this, most likely Homa or Yajna (fire ritual) to be performed,

In addition to these specific rituals, it is also important for the couple to maintain a pure and spiritual mindset throughout the conception process. This might involve practicing yoga, meditation, or other spiritual disciplines to help purify the mind and body.

It is important to note that the Garbhadana Samskara is not just for the couple's benefit but for the society as well. It is a reminder that the couple is taking on a very important role as parents, and it is their responsibility to bring up their child to be a good and responsible member of society.

The Garbhadana Samskara is an important ritual that helps to sanctify the act of conception and create a positive environment for the unborn child. It is also serves as a reminder of the spiritual responsibilities and duties that come with parenthood.

ᐅᐅᐅ

"India is the mother of all civilizations. India is the fountain of the world's cultures. India is the seed-ground of the world's religions." - Mahatma Gandhi

TWO

PUMSAVANA SAMSKARA

Pumsavana Samskara – is usually performed between the second and fourth month of pregnancy. Its purpose is: to insure the good health of the foetus and the proper formation of its organs, so that the family line and tradition will perpetuate thorugh the baby.

Pumsavana Samskara is a very important Hindu ritual which forms part of the 16 samskaras or rites of passage in the life of a Hindu. It is traditionally celebrated during the second and fourth month of pregnancy and is part of the rituals that form the Hindu Scriptures.

Pumsavana Samskara is observed in order to confer on the unborn child the blessings of physical, intellectual, psychological and spiritual health. During the ceremony, the father places his hand on the mother's belly in a gesture symbolizing his blessing and willingness to provide protection and care to the unborn child. The mother may then be anointed with turmeric or sandalwood and is presented with gifts of fruit and grains blessed by the priest who then utters auspicious mantras. The mantra recited by the priest is very important as it is believed to shape the destiny of the unborn child.

The Pumsavana Samskara ritual is followed around all parts of India, with slight variations, depending on the region and specific Hindu denomination. For example, in some parts of India, it is customary to sacrifice an animal, while in others, the entire ceremony is performed with no sacrifice. In some Hindu denominations, the mother may be anointed with honey or curd, or adorning herself with a special sacred thread.

Like any religious or traditional system, the Pumsavana Samskara rituals provides important socio-cultural benefits. It allows the Hindu community to practice their religious customs and traditions and also brings together family members, relatives, and friends to celebrate and welcome the unborn child in the family. The ceremony gives an insight into how the baby will be treated and looked after once it is born and it also serves as a symbol of respect for the baby's mother.

Pumsavana Samskara can be considered a unique and important tradition, which has been passed down through generations. It is considered a very auspicious beginning for the unborn child and is a reminder to all those around that the abortion of a fetus is not a practice to be tolerated. This traditional Hindu ceremony serves as an important reminder of the sanctity of life and of the need to provide the best possible care during pregnancy.

ᚦᚦᚦ

"India has a very rich culture, and we should
be proud of it." - Ratan Tata

THREE

SIMANTONNAYANA SAMSKARA

Simantonnayana Samskara, also known as "parting the hair," is one of the 16 samskaras in Hindu tradition. It is a ritual performed during the last trimester of pregnancy for the purpose of wishing for a safe delivery, similar to a baby shower. This is when simantonoyana Samskara is performed. Its purpose is to protect the foetus–especially its newly forming mind–from all negative influences, and also to stimulate the development of the unborn child's intellect.However, there is some disagreement among authorities as to whether this samskara should be performed only for the first child, or for every child.

Simantonoyana is one of the series of samskaras that mark different points during a person's life, including birth, marriage, and death. During this samskara, a pregnant woman's body is anointed with saffron paste, her hands are tied to signify a pledge to take care of the unborn child and she is given a sacred thread called the simanta. The priest will then conduct a puja, in which blessings are sought from the gods and the attending guests offer their appreciation and predictions of a healthy, happy baby.

It is believed that honoring this samskara is likely to prevent any difficulties in the woman's pregnancy. Traditional customs involve respecting seniors, eating healthily, and avoiding negative language and behavior. The woman and her family will also be encouraged to spend time in quiet contemplation and meditation and to ask for protection from divine forces for the unborn baby.

The ceremony reflects the spiritual importance of pregnancy in the lives of Hindu families, who regard it as a time of blessing, celebration, and joy. The pregnant woman is feted, thanked, and prayed for so that she and her unborn baby will be strong and healthy. After the ceremony, there are other similar rites like the jatakarma that are conducted at regular intervals. All of these added samskaras help to strengthen the bond between the family and the unborn child, ensuring the best possible start in life for the coming baby.

By performing the simantonoyana ceremony, new parents-to-be can honor the divine and ask for the positive reaffirmation that the pregnancy is proceeding well. It marks a time of heightened anticipation and joy for the new family, as both the woman and her baby are blessed, celebrated, and hosted with the sacred and age-old tradition of the samskara.

ᐅᐅᐅ

"India is the cradle of the human race, the birthplace of human speech, the mother of history, the grandmother of legend, and the great-grandmother of tradition." - Mark Twain

FOUR

JATAKARMA SAMSKARA

Jatakarma Samskara is the ritual performed at the birth of a child noting the birth time and star and thus create a birth chart which is suppose to be the blue print of ones life.

Jatakarma or 'birth ceremony' is an ancient Vedic ritual which is the commencement of the 16 traditional ceremonies (samskaras) in a Hindu Sanatan Dharma family. This ceremony is said to bring blessings from the Gods and is one of the highest honor accorded to a newborn child in Hinduism. Jatakarma is an important milestone for a baby's entry into the world tying them to the familial and communal hindu customs.

The traditional practice of Jatakarma is for the father, or other family members to make a purified space for a priest, who starts the ceremony with traditional mantras. Then the infant's forehead is symbolically marked with vermillion or a mixture of curd, ghee, honey and clarified butter. This is said to protect the newborn from evil spirits, and signify their entry into the community.

This ritual is often performed on the fifth or eleventh day after the birth. It is to be completed with the chanting of 'Jatakarmashanti' mantras and when completed parents bless the newly born life, asking the Gods to grace the baby with good health, happiness and prosperity. Jatakarma is especially important as it is one of the few "parvans" or meaningful events saved within Hindu clans and "gotras".

On this day, it is said that the Hindu God Vishnu becomes the guarantor for the child as a part of the ritual; it is believed that the soul of this unborn child has a cosmic origin and is a part of the universal source. Hence, all family members gather to pray for a bright and successful future of this newfound life.

Jatakarma rituals are more than just superstitions but have meaningful religious connotations. Jatakarma is a symbolic reminder that this young life will grow smarter, and stronger, and will learn about the religion and meaning of life. On that day, all signify that the main responsibility of the family is to protect and take care of this innocent soul and ensure that all his or her endeavors are only for the good of society and nation. Thus, this marks the beginning of a family's commitment in nurturing and growing this young life.

ᵱᵱᵱ

"India is a land of ancient culture and wisdom,
and these are qualities that cannot be easily
bought or sold." - Dalai Lama

FIVE

NAMAKARANA SAMSKARA

Namakarana Samskara – On the eleventh day after the child's birth, namakarana Samskara is performed. In this ceremony, the child receives its name.

Namakarana Samskara is one of sixteen Hindu spiritual ceremonies, referred to as samskaras, that are considered essential to a Hindu's religious growth and development. It marks the ritual of granting a name to a newborn baby and is said to be performed by parents and divine grace. This ceremony is believed to give the child an identity and helps to pave the way for the child's social, emotional and spiritual growth.

The Namakarana Samskara is commonly known to be performed on the tenth day of the birth of a child. Depending on the local customs, Hindu astrology and the parents' preference, the ritual is traditionally held anywhere from the sixth to twelfth day after the birth. There are several rituals associated with the ceremony, each with a spiritual significance, and many also include some form of ritual bathing.

On the day of the ritual, an elderly or priestly figure, such as a pundit or maharaj, is invited to the home or temple to perform the ceremony with mantras and yagnas. Before the ceremony, traditionally the ground is smeared with cow dung and in some regions, the dung is drawn out in the form of a swastika – a significant Hindu symbol. The baby is placed in the center of the swastika and the maharaj begins the ceremony.

The Namakarana Samskara calls for the invocation of Agni – the god of Fire, Vaayu – the god of Wind and Varuna – the god of Water. This is to give the child the grace and strength of three divine elements. The mantras chanted in this ceremony a few of the verses from Rig Veda and the parents and priests sing praises of the gods in order to invoke good and auspicious energy into the new child.

Following this, the baby is bathed in water that has been sanctified with mantras, rice, grass and other sacred items. As part of the ritual, the priest will whisper the chosen name into the child's ear without making it public. This is an important part of the ceremony as it is believed that by saying the name out loud, the power in the name is released and it will lose its spiritual power. After the name has been said, the priest sprinkles holy water or saffron water on the baby's head and offers flowers and grains. This marks the end of the Namakarana Samskara.

Namakarana Samskara is an important part of Hindu culture and is considered a rite of passage for a newborn baby. It marks the naming of the child and gives them an identity in society. This ceremony holds great spiritual significance as it is believed to bring prosperity and good fortune to the child and protect them from the ill effects of planetary combinations.

"India is a geographical term. It is no more a united nation than the Equator." - Winston Churchill

SIX

NISHKRAMANA SAMSKARA

Nishkramana Samskara - is an important Hindu ritual for the first outing of a newborn baby. This has been practiced since ancient times and is an important milestone in the baby's life. It marks the child's transition from the indoors to the great outdoors and ushers him/her into a lifelong journey of discovering the world.

The ritual is held a few weeks after the child's birth, but its exact dates and customs may differ across the country. The grandparents generally perform the ritual along with the help of a purohit or a priest who chants mantras and invokes blessings on the baby.

To begin the ritual, the baby is bathed and placed in a small carton or cradle. The father then takes the baby in his arms and takes him out of the house and carries him around the neighbourhood. The priest follows him, chanting mantras and showering the baby with grains or saying 'swaha' or 'swaha' with every step. This signifies that the baby is being showered with abundance, love, and protection.

When the father has taken the baby around the neighbourhood, the baby is brought back inside. He/she is then aarti-ed, or showered with blessings in the form of a lamp. Parents, grandparents and relatives participate in the aarti and shower the baby with warm blessings. The baby is then taken home and put to sleep in his/her cot.

In some Hindu families, child-naming rituals are also performed along with Nishkramana Samskara. After the aarti, the priest is invited to name the child. The parents choose a good name for the child and the priest pronounces it sacredly with mantras and blessings from the gods.

Nishkramana Samskara is a rite of passage and a blessing in the life of the new baby that is sure to bring him/her good luck and abundant joy. It is a traditional ritual, but as times and lifestyles change, modern families may also perform the ritual in their own way, as long as it is done with devotion and positive energy. Consequently, it remains an important and deeply meaningful Hindu custom that embraces the joy of a new addition to the family.

ᕼᕼᕼ

"The culture of India is the mother of all cultures, because it is old, because it sustains." - Jiddu Krishnamurti

SEVEN

ANNAPRASHANA SAMSKARA

Annaprashana Samskara – The first feeding of solid food to the baby, usually in the sixth month after birth.

Annaprashana Samskara is an important ritual observed in Hinduism, performed for the first time an infant has solid food. Annaprashana literally translates as "food consecration", and is done to bless the infant for sound health, growth and prosperity. Different regions of India observe the annaprashana ceremony in unique ways, as all follow different rituals, customs and activities.

At the start of the ceremony, the parents wash the baby's face and hands. Then they perform the pooja (ritual prayer to the gods) and offerings are made to the Gods, such as milk and honey. The date and time of the ceremony is chosen auspiciously and often involves all close members of the family or friends of the family, who will bring gifts for the child and celebrate. According to the Hindu tradition, the child's head is shaved or adorned with holy threads marking the special occasion.

The main event of the Annaprashana ceremony is the offering of the first solid food to the infant. This is usually a balanced diet of rice, jaggery and various other cereals and pulses. It is often recommended to choose grains of three different colors (red, yellow, and black) that symbolize the three deities, Brahma, Vishnu and Maheshwara. In some cases, instead of cooked food, the parents give the infant honey. Depending on regional rituals, the infant is offered food with either gold or silver spoon.

In addition to the food, various items such as raw rice and different colored Gud (jaggery) are also given to the baby while reciting special mantras. After that, the godparents bless the child with a long and healthy life and break a coconut in front of the baby. This signifies a healthy and prosperous life for the baby.

At the end of the ceremony, the child is dressed and decorated with traditional Hindu jewelry and a Tilak or Bindi is applied to the forehead of the infant. Alternatively, Haldi (turmeric) and Kumkum is smeared on the infant's forehead. The relatives and family then take part in a lavish feast and traditional music and dancing making the celebration of Annaprashana a joyful affair.

Annaprashana marks a major milestone in the life of an infant and the ceremony is performed with love and devotion to bless them for their life ahead.

ॐॐॐ

"India is not a country of the Hindus only. It is a country of the Muslims, the Christians and the Parsees too. It is the land of Islam and Buddhism, of Siva and Vishnu." - Mahatma Gandhi

EIGHT

KARNAVEDHA SAMSKARA

Karnavedha Samskara – usually performed in the sixth or seventh month after birth, consists of the piercing of the baby's ear lobes, so earrings may be worn.

Karnavedha Samskara is an Indian Vedic ritual that marks the beginning of a child's life. It is a rite of passage celebrated when a baby is six to twelve months old, and it marks the ceremonial piercing of the baby's ear. In Hindu culture, both the father and grandfather play a major role in the ceremony, as the Vedic scriptures proclaim that the father is responsible for conducting and attending the ritual for their son, and for the grandfather for his grandson.

The ritual is often preceded by the preparation of traditional items such as holy water, food items, and clothes. Families may also conduct poojas or prayers, and invite priests to read verses from the Vedas. During the actual ritual, the baby's ear is pierced with a specially designed needle or blade, usually made of brass. While a clove or nut is usually used as a marker to choose the correct spot, the selected point depends on whether the baby is a boy or a girl. The father or grandfather then steps forward to invoke blessings of Gods and Goddesses, such as Ganesha, Vishnu, Surya, and Shiva. He then pours the holy water over the baby's head and ties an amulet to his wrist.

The parents may then place earrings, as per their religious belief, in the baby's ears. If the family wishes, a priest can also perform a mantra chanting ceremony. The newly created hole is often anointed with vermilion and red sandalwood paste for the baby's health and prosperity. Friends and relatives gatherings are conducted, where gifts and sweets are given to the new family member. The family is often considered to enter in a new stage of life with this special ceremony, as the baby was believed to have been given life with physical manifestation.

In some parts of India, Karnavedha Samskara is complete with a naming ceremony. The name is usually selected from Hindu astrology, which is believed to be auspicious. Other rituals, such as the initiation of a sacred thread or the bestowal of religious books or icon to the baby, can also be done as part of this ceremony.

Karnavedha Samskara is a ceremony that marks the beginning of a baby's life, and it is an important ritual in Hindu culture. It is steeped in tradition and is an occasion for families to come together and celebrate the new family member. It is a symbolic way of providing the new life with protection, health, prosperity, and blessings.

"India is the land of spirituality, and the spiritual teachings of India have been a source of inspiration for the entire world." - Sri Sri Ravi Shankar

NINE

CHUDAKARANA SAMSKARA

Chudakarana Samskara – At the end of the first year after birth, or during the third year, the child's hair is shaved–all but a tuft on the top of the head. This ritual shaving of hair, performed with ceremony, prayers, and chanting of Vedic hymns, is chudakarana Samskara This Samskara is for both boys and girls.

Chudakarana Samskara, ritual and other activities, is an important ritual observed in Hindu tradition. The Sanskrit word 'Chudakarana' means 'the rite of initiating'. This ritual is generally performed for male children on the sixth or eighth day after birth. It marks the child's initiation into the Hindu faith.

The main activity in Chudakarana Samskara is the Shuddhi or purification of the child, usually done by sprinkling or pouring sacred waters on the body of the baby. The traditional priest then soaks the child's head in water while chanting mantras, followed by the tying of a tuft, which is a lock of hair, at the back of the baby's head. While tying, the priest usually says, "Let this tuft be a sign of your auspicious, prosperous and happy life".

Apart from the Shuddhi and tuft tying, there are other rituals and activities involved in the Chudakarana Samskara . These may include the introduction of the child to God and taking His blessings, seek the parents' permission for the new name of the child, and the tantric ceremony to protect the child from evil.

Traditionally, a feast is organized for the family members, along with their close relatives and friends. People wear traditional attires and the baby is decorated with jewelry, new clothes, and ornaments. The priest recites mantras, chants prayers and performs the religious rites. During the ceremony, the guests are served with sweets and beverages as a part of the joyous occasion.

This Hindu ritual of Chudakarana is an important tradition which not only marks the initiation of the child into the Hindu faith, but also celebrates the parents' first successful task of raising a new life in their family. It is a beginning of a new journey in life, and a reminder of the love and strength of religious values. Apart from that, Chudakarana is also an occasion for the family members to come closer and share their happiness.

ÞÞÞ

"India is the one country in the world where spiritualism and science are not in conflict." - Dr. APJ Abdul Kalam

TEN

VIDYARAMBHA SAMSKARA

Vidyarambha Samskara – begins a student's primary education by ceremonially introducing the child to the alphabet.

Vidyarambha Samskara, also known as Akshara Sweekaram, is an important ritual in the Hindu tradition. It marks the beginning of the formal education of a child and is usually performed between the ages of four and six. This ritual signifies the initiation of a child's education into the field of life and is a symbolic blessing to the child for his/her academic success and intellectual development.

The ritual is a very traditional and elaborate affair. On the day of the ritual, the child is adorned in traditional clothes and jewelry and all the invited family and friends are also dressed in their finest. Initially, the ritual begins with an invocation to Goddess Saraswathi and the presiding priest reads prayers which are recited aloud by everyone present. In the next step, an edible paste made of rice and turmeric is placed in front of Goddess Saraswathi's idol. The priest then teaches the child the first Sanskrit letters of the alphabet, with each letter being marked with a pinch of the same paste onto the child's hand. The kid is then made to attempt to repeat the syllables as an act of homage to the goddess of learning.

The Vidyarambha Samskara is completed with the chanting of significant verses from the Vedas and the distribution of prasadam followed by the distribution of gifts to the child. Typically, these gifts include books, stationery, and other educational items to symbolize the importance of the event for the child and encourage the child to be a great learner.

At the completion of the ritual, the child is considered to have officially begun his or her academic journey. Throughout the ceremony, the child's guardians and family members shower him or her with their blessings and prayers for a bright and successful future.

In India, Vidyarambha Samskara, is seen as an essential step in the life of a Hindu and is traditionally celebrated with fervor. It is believed to be a great omen that will bring success in the child's school life. The event is a reminder that the Vedas and Hindu literature are the foundation of life and that continuous growth of knowledge is essential for personal and communal development.

ᏞᏞᏞ

"India is the land of the Vedas, the Upanishads, the Puranas, the Ramayana and the Mahabharata. It is the land where the Bhagavad Gita was written and where the Buddha attained enlightenment." - Dalai Lama

ELEVEN

UPANAYANA SAMSKARA

Upanayana Samskara – initiates the formal study of the Vedas. It is one of the most important and esteemed of the samskaras. Upon performance of Upanayana, a boy traditionally moves from home to live in the ashram of the guru.

The Upanayana Samskara ceremony takes place when a child reaches the age of eight or eleven. The child symbolically learns the Vedas through the Yagya offered to him by a source of knowledge, known as the guru. During this ceremony, the guru ties a sacred thread called Yagnopavitam around the neck of the child. This sacred thread symbolizes the boy's entry into the disciplined lifestyle and practice of studying the Vedas.

Furthermore, this ceremony includes many other rituals such as painting the head of the boy or putting a tilak on his forehead. During the time of this ceremony, the family of the boy showers him with love and blessings. They also offer him gifts such as cows, gold and monetary gifts. After the ceremony, the boy is directed to learn about the Vedas and perform traditional rituals under his guru's guidance.

Along with the samskara, there are other important activities that take place during this ceremony. The boy is taught to meditate and chant mantras during the ceremony. This process of reflection assists in his spiritual journey and helps clear the individual's mind in order to move and transition into a higher level of consciousness.

In addition, the ceremony also focuses on physical activities. The boy is taught to offer prayers to deities and learn about the Hindu culture by reciting mantras, scriptures, and performing Homam. By doing these rituals, he gradually grows into an integral part of the traditional community and learns to take on his responsibilities as a man.

The Upanayana Samskara is an important Hindu tradition that is highly esteemed in India. It is believed to have originated in ancient times, and teaches the boy the importance of spirituality, value system and Hindu Sanatan Dharma. Although, in recent times, the traditional system of Upanayana Samskara has seen some modifications, it still remains an indispensable part of Indian culture.

ॐॐॐ

"India is a living example of how different cultures, religions and ways of life can coexist in harmony." - Ratan Tata

TWELVE

SAMAVARTANA SAMSKARA

Samavartana Samskara – With samavartana Samskara the disciple graduates from his Vedic studies and returns from the house of his guru. Thereafter, the disciple will marry and raise a family, and so enter the stage of householder, grihasthashrama.

Samavartana, also known as Upanayana, is one of the sixteen major samskaras or ritual ceremonies in Hinduism. It marks the end of Brahmacharya (studenthood), which is the period of discipline and schooling during which the Vedas, a collection of sacred Hindu scriptures, are studied in detail. It is usually performed between the ages of 18 -21 as a sign of youth's successful completion of the celibate studenthood phase.

The Samavartana Samskara is a joyous celebratory event that is often conducted in temples. During the ceremony, after an invocation of the gods, the youth is presented with new clothing, ornaments, and valuable gifts. At this time, the young person will also receive a new name and leave behind their celibate studenthood identity. He or she is then anointed with the holy water of the Ganges and walk across a ruler laid on the floor symbolizing their departure from studenthood and entrance into the realm of responsible adulthood.

After the ceremony, there is a procession that includes singing, dancing, and the offering of Tarpana, which are customary oblations made to the gods and ancestors. Friends and family members of the person coming-of-age engage in traditional games, such as throwing coloured powder and singing and dancing. The day ends with a grand feast that all those present take part in.

The Samavartana Samskara signifies the entry of the individual into responsible adulthood and the beginning of their journey into Dharma (righteousness). This ritual is a reminder that the purpose of life is to be dutiful and practice virtuous acts to benefit mankind. After the completion of this event, the individual embarks on a journey of marriage, children, and various spiritual, educational and professional pursuits.

The Samavartana Samskara is a significant religious ceremony that is believed to empower the individual with the knowledge, values, and character needed to achieve their goals in life. The ritual itself is a sacred event that celebrates one's growth into adulthood and marks the beginning of the journey of self-discovery and maturity.

ppp

"The spiritual heritage of India is one of the most valuable treasures of human history, and it continues to inspire and guide humanity today." - Jiddu Krishnamurti

THIRTEEN

VIVAHA SAMSKARA

Vivaha Samskara – The traditional Hindu wedding ceremony is known as vivaha Samskara It is considered by many to be the most important of all the samskaras.

The union of a man and a woman in virtuous matrimony is viewed as a most sacred identity in the sociocultural milieu of India. This union is celebrated in the process of Vivaha Samskara, which is a Sanskrit term that means marriage rituals. These rituals are a blend of traditional customs, along with other activities entailed to inaugurate a life-long commitment and responsibility between two individuals who are about to venture into an unknown form of journey.

In India, Vivaha Samskara is not just about two individuals entering into an association, but is about two families coming together as one. This union is viewed as a rite of passage, in which the two families partake in preparing the couples for their upcoming married life. At the heart of these rituals lies the emphasis of reciting mantras and performing havans (sacrificial offering). Over the generations, nuptial ceremonies have gone a complete revamp with the changing trends; however, many of the rituals and customs remain similar to the ancient Vedic and puranic texts.

The marriage ceremonies, usually a two-three day event, starts off with the performing of particular ceremonies, to concentrate spiritual and mental energy of the couple. As per Hindu customs, the Hanuman Puja is performed, followed by Sankalpam (pledge). Then, the main rituals follow, with Mangala Snaanam (holy bath), followed by that, the Kashi Yatra, in which the groom symbolically leaves home to live a spiritual journey. The wedding then moves on to the Jeevakaalasam ritual enjoining the couple in matrimonial bond, through the tying of the Mangala Sutra (necklace of auspicious marriage) Also, the traditional Madhuparkam ritual is performed, as holy offerings of milk, rice and honey, to signify the union of two souls in love.

The wedding ceremony is concluded with a grand reception, known as Vidaai, an emotional farewell of the bride with the family, signifying her arrivial to her new home. The post-wedding rituals include Graha Pradhanam, where the couples is welcomed by the in-laws by an aarti, with sweet offerings. This ritual is followed by a feast, called Grihapravesham, conducted at the groom's home, as a embarkment of their married life. Vivah Samskara also include other rituals such as Satyanarayan Puja and a seven-day turmeric ceremony, as part of blessings and a prosperous life ahead.

Vivah Samskara is a much revered sacrament that ensures the safe and secure union of a man and a woman. It is a momentous occasion for two families to join together in their new endeavor. These rituals are steeped in traditional customs, and serve as a lifetime reminder of their marriage vows and commitment.

"The spiritual tradition of India is one of the most ancient in the world, and it continues to inspire and guide people today." - Sri Sri Ravi Shankar

FOURTEEN

PANCHA MAHA YAJNA SAMSKARA

Panchamahayagna Samskara – A married couple performs the panchamahayajna, or five great sacrifices, daily. In this Samskara, one honours, in turn, the rishis, the gods, the parents, humankind, and all created beings.

The Panchamahayagna Samskara is one of the most important and widely celebrated rituals in Hindu culture. It holds a special place in the Hindu tradition of carrying out various spiritual activities with the help of divine forces. This ritual is the key to getting closer to the higher powers and achieving inner bliss.

The Panchamahayagna Samskara is a combination of five separate activities that make up the complete ritual. The first activity is called 'Grihapravesh' and this is the entrance of a new member into the house. The family members perform a prayer ritual to invite spiritual powers in. They then offer flowers, rice, and fruits to them and seek their blessings for the whole family.

The second activity of the Panchamahayagna Samskara is known as 'Annaprashan' or the feeding of the first grains to a new born baby. The family members offer a sweet mixture of rice, ghee, and sugar called 'Annam' to the baby and offer it to the gods. This is done to bless the baby with good health and long life.

The third activity of the Panchamahayagna Samskara is called 'Namakarana' or the naming ceremony of the baby. This ceremony is considered as very auspicious and the baby is given a new name as it is a very special occasion. The parents seek the blessings of deities for the welfare of the child.

The fourth activity is 'Upanayana'. This ceremony is conducted for boys when they are 8 years old. This is a very important event in which the parents give two pieces of cotton thread or string to the boy and ask him to wear it around his neck and waist. This ceremony is important in shaving the path of knowledge. The fifth activity of Panchamahayagna Samskara is 'Vivah' which is the marriage ceremony. During this ceremony the couple ties their knot of love and this union is considered to be full of very positive energy.

The Panchamahayagna Samskara is a very important ritual and is considered as a bridge between earthly life and the divine realm. It is performed to seek the blessings of gods and goddesses and to ensure the peace, prosperity and good fortune of a family. All these activities are performed to purify the minds and souls of those participating. They bring about a feeling of togetherness, humility, and spiritual connection among all those present. This shows the importance of Panchamahayagna Samskara and how it helps to bring the family closer to their divine power.

"The culture of India is a rich mixture of tradition, spirituality, and modernity." - Ratan Tata

FIFTEEN

VANAPRASTHA SAMSKARA

Vanaprastha Samskara – According to the Vedic tradition, vanaprastha is the third stage of life, following brahmacharya (Vedic student/disciple) and grihasta (householder). Here, a one leaves behind ones life in the world and retires to the forest (or serving the society), to live an ascetic life devoted to service, study of the scriptures and to meditation.

Vanaprastha Samskara is one of the four stages, or "samskaras", in the traditional Hindu system of life. These samskaras are: brahmacharya, grihastha, vanaprastha, and sannyasa. Vanaprastha marks the transition between the active and the contemplative life that is necessary to move toward spiritual advancement.

Vanaprastha begins at the age of around 50 or 55, when a person leaves the Grihastha stage of life and starts to focus more on spiritual pursuits. This period of transition is marked by a variety of rituals and activities.

First, a fire sacrifice, known as Homa, is performed. This is meant to signify the transition of the individual into a more spiritually focused life. Following this, the individual announces his intention to undergo vanaprastha and is formally blessed with the title of Vanaprastha.

Next, the individual begins the process of cultivating certain spiritual qualities known as "Virtues of Vanaprastha". These virtues include universal love and compassion, contentment and self-reliance, humility and forgiveness, devotion to God, and respect for one's elders. During this period, the individual begins to practice meditation, yoga and other spiritual disciplines that will help them prepare for the transition to life as a sannyasi.

Other ritualistic activities associated with vanaprastha include the daily performance of a Puja (worship ritual) at sunrise and sunset. During this ritual, offerings are made to the gods and mantras are chanted. In addition, the individual will receive special teachings from a guru or spiritual teacher that will help him move toward enlightenment.

Finally, it is customary for vanaprasthas to travel to various pilgrimage sites and holy shrines. It is believed that doing so will add even more spiritual value to the transition from grihastha to sannyasa.

Vanaprastha is an important transition period in the traditional Hindu system of life. During it, individuals are encouraged to practice certain spiritual activities and rituals that will help them progress along their spiritual path. These activities can range from simple prayers and meditations, to more elaborate rituals such as Homa and Puja. By engaging in these practices, individuals are able to gain spiritual merit and make valuable progress toward their goal of sannyasa.

ᕬᕬᕬ

"The spiritual heritage of India is the most precious treasure that mankind possesses." - Swami Vivekananda

SIXTEEN

ANTYESHTI SAMSKARA

Antyeshti Samskara – The final sacrament, the funeral rites, are known as antyeshti Samskara.

Antyeshti Samskara is a ceremony observed in Hinduism where the final rites are performed for departed souls that are considered to be the most important of all life-cycle rituals. This ceremony is conducted in order to release the soul from worldly connections, to ensure that the soul can attain a good afterlife. This ceremony is usually performed in recognition of death and the sentiment of loss and grief that accompanies it.

It is usually carried out by a priest who is responsible for the rituals and accompanied by family of the deceased as well as relatives and friends. The priest begins by chanting mantras as per Vedic protocol, followed by offerings such as ghee, flowers, fruits and sandalwood paste. A vessel filled with water is placed near the body to be burnt and its five elements - earth, air, fire, water and ether- are annointed.

The priest then performs various rituals such as the Praan Pratishtha ritual, demonstrating that the vital force of the soul residing in the body has been shifted to the new plane of afterlife.

Subsequently, the body is bathed and clothed in clean white dhotis, wrapped in saffron cloth, and then placed on the Manpapatra or a bamboo cot. The cot is decorated with flowers and garlands and the eldest son or the closest relative of the deceased is expected to carry it. Prayers are recited, and homage is paid to the departed soul. Once the body is cremated and the ashes are collected, a memorial service is held for the dead. The ashes, called 'Aasheervad', are then cast away in an auspicious part of a holy river or sea.

The grieving family of the departed conduct special rituals and activities in order to help the deceased to have a better transit to the afterlife. Prayers and donations are made to Gods and Goddesses, sacred mantras are recited to drive away negative energies, and a proper feast is offered in the honour of the deceased. The family members and other relatives then partake of the food as a sign of attachment to the departed soul.

Antyeshti Samskara is one of the most important ceremonies in Hinduism and encompasses the rituals and activities that are designed to honour the departed soul and enable a better afterlife for the dead. It is conducted with a lot of reverence and participants usually view it as a way to provide solace and comfort to their departed relatives.

ᐽᐽᐽ

Other Books Of The Author

1. The Moments When I Met God
2. Kashiyile Theertha Pathangal
3. GURU GYAN VANI
4. Abhiprerak Gita
5. ASSI SE JAIN GHAT TAK
6. Hopelessness of Arjuna
7. The Soul and It's True Nature
8. Sense of Action (Karma)
9. Action through Wisdom
10. Action through Wisdom
11. THEORY AND PRACTICAL OF EVERY ACTION
12. LOGICAL UNDERSTANDING OF THE SUPREME
13. THE IMPERISHABLE SUPREME
14. Yatra Nishadraj se Hanuman Ghat Tak
15. Yatra Karnatak Ghat se Raja Ghat Tak
16. Yatra Pandey Ghat se Prayagraj Ghat Tak
17. Yatra Ranjendra Prasad Ghat se Dattatreya Ghat Tak
18. YaatraSindhiya Ghat se Gwaliar Ghat Tak
19. Yatra Mangala Gauri Ghat se Hanuman Gadhi Ghat Tak
20. Yatra Gaay Ghat Se Nishad Ghat Tak
21. MAA GANGA, GHATEN EVM UTSAV
22. Ganga Arti Dev Deepavali evam Any Utsav
23. Potentials of Digitalized India
24. VEDIC CONSCIOUSNESS
25. A Brief Introduction to Vedic Science
26. Kashi ke Barah Jyotirling
27. IMPACT OF MOTIVATION
28. Let's have a Milky Way Journey
29. Color Therapy in a Nutshell

30. Rigveda in a Nutshell
31. Yajurveda in a Nutshell
32. Samveda in a Nutshell
33. Atharva Veda in a Nutshell
34. Ayushman Bhava - Ayurveda
35. Srimad Bhagavad Gita and Upanishad Connection
36. Srimad Bhagavad Gita - an attempt to summarize each chapter.
37. Facts and Impact of Nakshatra
38. Astro Gems - NAVARATNA
39. Ekadashi - A Concise Overview
40. A Concise View of Hanuman Chalisa
41. Inspirational Gita
42. Nakshatraranyam
43. Summary of 18 Mahapuranas
44. Synopsis of 18 Upa Puranas
45. Rigvediya Upanishads
46. Shukla Yajurvediya Upanishads
47. Krishna Yajurvediya Upanishads
48. Samavediya Upanishads
49. Atharvavediya Upanishads
50. The Seven Great Sages
51. From Rocket Scientist to President Dr. APJ Abdul Kalam
52. The Visionary's Voice - Quotes of Dr. APJ Abdul Kalam
53. The Wisdom of Swami Vivekananda: Insights and Inspiration from a Legendary Spiritual Teacher
54. Ayurvedic Remedies from the Garden
55. Sages and Seers
56. Rising Strong – Motivational Stories of Women
57. Beyond Flames -Mystery stories of Funeral Ghat Manikarnika
58. The Origins of Tulsi: A Look at the Mythological Roots of the Plant"

ppp

Contact

DR. JAGADEESH PILLAI

PhD in Vedic Science

Four Times Guinness World Record Holder

Winner of Mahatma Gandhi Vishwa Shanti Puraskar and
Global Peace Ambassador

Gemology, Astro & Vastu Consultant - Spiritual Counselor

Consultant for designing World Record Ideas

Efficient Tarot Card Reader

9839093003

myrichindia@gmail.com

drjagadeeshpillai@facebook

drjagadeeshpillai@instagram

jagadeeshpillai@youtube

www. JAGADEESHPILLAI.com

ᗑᗑᗑ

|| LOKAHA SAMASTHAHA SUKHINO BHAVANTU ||

• 83 •